MW00721126

THE LITTLE
GREY FLANNEL BOOK

THE LITTLE GREY FLANNEL BOOK

Quotations on Men

Compiled, Annotated
& Introduced by

OLINE LUINENBURG
& STEPHEN OSBORNE

A LITTLE RED BOOK
PULP PRESS BOOK PUBLISHERS

A LITTLE RED BOOK

THE LITTLE GREY FLANNEL BOOK:
QUOTATIONS ON MEN

Copyright ©1991
by Arsenal Pulp Press Ltd.
All Rights Reserved
ISBN 0-88978-238-5

CIP Data: See page 6
LITTLE RED BOOKS ARE
PUBLISHED BY
PULP PRESS BOOK PUBLISHERS
1062 Homer Street #100
Vancouver BC V6B 2W9
A Division of Arsenal Pulp Press Ltd.

Cover: Kelly Brooks
Typesetting: Vancouver Desktop
Publishing Centre
Printing: Continental Printing
Printed and bound in the U.S.A.

TABLE OF CONTENTS

CANADIAN CATALOGUING
IN PUBLICATION DATA

Main entry under title:
The Little grey flannel book
(A Little red book)
Includes index.
  ISBN 0-88978-239-3
  1. Men—Quotations.   2.Men—
Humor   3. Quotations, English.
I. Luinenburg, Oline, 1962-
II. Osborne, J. S. (James Stephen), 1947-
III. Series.
PN6084.M4L58 1991   305.31'0207
C91-091638-1

This volume appears as a companion to *The Little Pink Book (Quotations on Women)*, and may be said to have been invoked by that first, perhaps more urgent, work, whose effect we hoped might be to assist readers wishing to avoid the repetition of certain themes in history. With the recent surge of media interest in the phenomenon of the "men's movement," we turned our researches to this interesting subject, to discover therein a surprising consistency in the position of men in our culture's history. So that here we find fewer varieties of insight, and more variations on a theme. These variations at times tend toward increasing refinement; for example, the windier phrasings of another age found in, say, Teddy Roosevelt, are to be heard again in a purer, more haiku-like form, when we get to Roy Rogers.

This tendency is not surprising. Men having held the power for so long, any remark pertaining to them tends to reflect that position of power, even while seeming to question it. No doubt there lies a dialectic here, just beyond our ability to articulate it—and for that reason we, like so many of the sources quoted in these pages, are apt to jump into metaphor for explanation or, at least, some species of mental relief.

We might say, for example, that these two volumes—the pink and the grey—represent two sides of the same coin. But that would be misleading, if only because we cannot say who owns the coin. Assembling this volume we have learned this much: metaphors are made to delight, which is why they are so well suited to poetry; but only rarely do they instruct. With that caveat, then, we commend you to these pages, to the voices—and the whispers—of history.

SOURCES

Sources include (short titles given): *Bartlett's Familiar Quotations*. *Best of Bridge*. *Best of Trudeau*. *Book of Quotes*, Barbara Rowes. *Boswell's Life of Johnson*. *Choice of Heroes*, Mark Gerzon. *Contemporary Quotations*, James Simpson. *Dictionary of Outrageous Quotations*, C.R.S. Marsden. *Dictionary of Proverbs*, Petros D. Baz. *Fathers: A Collection*, Alexandra Towle. *Fitzhenry & Whiteside Book of Quotations*. *Colombo's Canadian Quotations*, John Robert Columbo. *Great Business Quotations*, Rolf B. White. *Hearts of Men*, Barbara Ehrenreich. *Home Book of Humourous Quotations*, A.K. Adams. *John Robert Colombo's Popcorn in Paradise*. *Men: An Investigation*, Phillip Hodson. *Morrow's International Dictionary of Contemporary Quotations*, Jonathan Green. *Newsweek*. *Penguin Dictionary of Modern Humourous Quotations*. *Penguin Dictionary of Quotations*, M.J. Cohen. *People*. *Quentin Crisp's Book of Quotations*. *Quotable Quotations Book*, Alec Lewis. *Royal Quotes*, Noel St. George. *Saturday Night*. *Say It Again*, Dorothy Uris. *Since You Ask Me*, Ann Landers. *Unnatural Quotations*, Leigh W. Rutledge. *Who Said What When*. *Vanity Fair*. *Whole Grains*, Art Speigelman.

OKAY, SO WHO'S GOING TO GET THE BALL ROLLING HERE?

An old man in a house is a good sign.   *—ancient proverb*

ON GETTING CLOSE TO THE MAN WITHIN

Next to man is his underwear.   *—Calgary Bob Edwards*

STRAINS OF THAT CHEERFUL ANCESTRAL MUSIC

Man is a little soul carrying around a corpse.   *—Greek proverb*

STILL SEARCHING FOR THAT ELUSIVE METAPHOR

Man is a rope connecting animal and superman.   *—Nietzsche*

WELL, IT'S A START, ANYWAY

Manners make the man.

—proverb

ON WHAT COUNTS

It's not the men in my life that count;
it's the life in my men.

—Mae West

LET'S TRY TO GET IT
INTO A NUTSHELL

And a woman is only a woman, but
a good cigar is a smoke.

—Rudyard Kipling

WELL, MAYBE NOT *ALL* THE TIME

Sometimes a cigar is just a cigar.

—Sigmund Freud

ON BEING SIX OF ONE OR HALF A DOZEN OF WHATEVER

A man without a wife is but half a man.   —*proverb*

BUT NOT THE ONLY WAY OF LOOKING AT IT

A woman without a man is like a fish without a bicycle.

—*Gloria Steinem*

ON THE FELLOWSHIP OF MEN

All men are alike in the light.

—*Anonymous*

A RATHER MORE APOCALYPTIC VIEW

Every man in this world needs a Zsa Zsa.   —*Zsa Zsa Gabor*

ON EFFICIENCY AND MALE SHREWDNESS

Male chauvinism is a shrewd method of extracting the maximum of work for the minimum of compensation.

—Michael Korda

AND THEY'RE NOT THE ONLY ONES

I owe every woman in America an apology.

—Larry Flynt, publisher of Hustler

GETTING THAT METAPHOR RIGHT MAY NOT BE SO EASY

Men are beasts, and even beasts don't behave as they do.

—Brigitte Bardot

ON THE ULTIMATE LOVE POTION, BEFORE CELLULAR PHONES

Power is the ultimate aphrodisiac.
—*Henry Kissinger*

ON THE SIDE EFFECTS OF THE ULTIMATE APHRODISIAC

The men who really wield, retain, and covet power are the kind who answer bedside phones while making love.

—*Nicholas Pileggi*

ON THE EVOLUTION OF CULTURES BASED IN CITIES

The major civilizing force in the world is not religion, it's sex.
—*Hugh Hefner*

ON THE PLEASURE PRINCIPAL
IN CIVILIZATION

No civilized man ever regrets a pleasure, and no uncivilized man ever knows what a pleasure is.

—*Oscar Wilde*

ON THERE BEING NOWHERE,
REALLY, TO HIDE

Probably the only place where a man can feel really secure is in a maximum security prison, except for the imminent threat of release.

—*Germaine Greer*

WELL, MAYBE WE'RE GETTING A
LITTLE CLOSER

What is a man? A miserable little pile of secrets.

—*André Malraux*

COME ON STANLEY, NO CHEAP SHOTS

Man isn't a noble savage, he's an ignoble savage.

—Stanley Kubrick

ON HAVING IT ALL AND KNOWING WHAT TO DO WITH IT

I do nothing that a man of unlimited funds, superb physical endurance and maximum scientific knowledge could not do.   *—Batman*

SOME THINGS JUST NEVER CHANGE

A gentleman of our days is one who has money enough to do what every fool would do if he could afford it: consume without producing.

—George Bernard Shaw

ON DEEPER IMPLICATIONS OF THE JAMES BOND ROLE MODEL

He smoked like Peter Lorre and drank like Humphrey Bogart and ate like Sydney Greenstreet and used up girls like Errol Flynn and then went out to a steam bath and came back looking like Clark Gable. It was all so reassuring that we never stopped to think that all these people are dead.   —*Harry Reasoner*

ON THE MALE LIBIDO AS THE SOFT-DRINK MACHINE OF THE PSYCHE

Male sexual response is far brisker and more automatic: it is triggered easily by things, like putting a quarter in a vending machine.

—*Alex Comfort*

ON WHAT MIGHT BE
AT THE ROOT OF
THE PROBLEM

Men are not given awards and promotions for bravery in intimacy.

—Gail Sheehy

ANCIENT WISDOM
RECONSIDERED

Early to rise and early to bed makes a man healthy and wealthy and dead.

—James Thurber

NOT TO SET IMPOSSIBILY HIGH
STANDARDS, THAT IS

I like men to behave like men— strong and childish.

—Francoise Sagan

ON BEHAVING LIKE A MAN

I'm goin' to stand up for America
until somebody shoots me.

—Roy Rogers

ON VALIDATION AND EXPRESSION

I'd never seen men hold each other.
I thought the only things they were
allowed to do was shake hands or
fight. *—Rita Mae Brown*

ON VALIDATION AND EXPRESSION
AT THE MOST BASIC LEVEL

Manhood at the most basic level can
be validated and expressed only in
action.

—George Gilder

ON ACHIEVING EARLY MIDDLE AGE

Men who are 'orthodox' when they

are young are in danger of being middle-aged all their lives.

—*Walter Lippman*

ON SEPARATING THE SOMETHING FROM THE SOMETHING OR OTHERS

The difference between men and boys is the price of their toys.

—*Liberace*

ON THE CORRECTNESS OF GETTING MARRIED AT ANY COST

If you cannot catch a bird of paradise, better take a wet hen.

—*Nikita Kruschev*

SOMEWHERE BETWEEN A ROCK AND A HARD PLACE

Men are always ready to respect anything that bores them.
> —*Marilyn Monroe*

THE CONNUBIAL CONTRADICTION ILLUMINATED

Marriage makes you legally half a person, and what man wants to live with half a person?   —*Gloria Steinem*

ON TAKING BACK HALF ONE'S LIFE

I'm officially resigning as the prime minister's wife.   —*Margaret Trudeau*

ON FULFILLING THE GRAND AMERICAN DREAM

I'm going to buy a castle and live like any other G.I.   —*Elvis Presley*

ON ANGST, GREY FLANNEL STYLE

A man's home is his hassle.
> —*Paul D. Arnold*

ON MARRIAGE AND THE
CONSUMER LIFE

Marrying a man is like buying something you've been admiring for a long time in a shop window. You may love it when you get home, but it doesn't always go with everything else in the house.

> —*Jean Kerr*

ON THE BODY-MIND DUALITY

There are some girls who are turned on by my body and some others who are turned off. But for the majority I just use it as a conversation piece. Like someone walking a cheetah down Forty-second Street would have a natural conversation piece.

—*Arnold Schwarzenegger*

ON A MORE RHETORICAL NOTE, MAYBE IN C, F AND G7

How many roads must a man walk down before you can call him a man?   —*Bob Dylan*

ON THERE BEING SOME HOPE FOR THE AVERAGE MAN

The average man is more interested in a woman who is interested in him than he is in a woman—any woman—with beautiful legs.

—*Marlene Dietrich*

ON THERE BEING VERY LITTLE HOPE FOR WHAT NORMAL MEN THERE ARE LEFT

Normal men have killed perhaps 100,000,000 of their fellow normal men in the last fifty years.

—R. D. Laing

FIRST THOUGHTS ON THE QUESTION OF ENTERING PUBLIC LIFE

I'm thinking about entering politics—I'd love to do it. But I haven't got the right wife.

—Mick Jagger

SECOND THOUGHTS ON STAYING IN PUBLIC LIFE

As usual, there's a great woman behind every idiot. *—John Lennon*

MORE ON THE SUPERMAN SYNDROME

I always had a repulsive sort of need to be something more than human.
—*David Bowie*

THOUGHTS ON IMMUTABILITY (DOES IT WORK BOTH WAYS?)

It's impossible for a woman to be married to the same man for 50 years. After the first 25, he's not the same man.   —*Farmer's Almanac, 1966*

ON HOW VALUE IS DETERMINED BY THE INEXORABLE LAW OF SUPPLY AND DEMAND

One good husband is worth two good wives; for the scarcer things are, the more they are valued.
—*Benjamin Franklin*

ON HOW GOODNESS FOLLOWS
FROM PARSIMONY

Some men are good because they find it cheaper than being wicked.
—*Calgary Bob Edwards*

ON THE DESCENT OF MAN

Mankind fell in Adam, and has been falling ever since, but it never touched bottom till it got to Henry Ward Beecher.   —*Tom Appleton*

AND THE EVOLUTION
OF SPECIES

The human species, according to the best theory I can form of it, is composed of two distinct races, the men who borrow and the men who lend.

—*Charles Lamb*

ALTHOUGH PERHAPS NOT YET FULLY ASCERTAINED

Man is more courageous, pugnacious and energetic than woman, and has a more inventive genius. His brain is absolutely larger, but whether or not proportionately to his larger body, has not, I believe, been fully ascertained.

—Charles Darwin

ANCIENT NOTES ON THE SURVIVAL OF THE NOT-SO-DUMB-AS-YOU-THINK

The male is more courageous than the female, and more sympathetic in the way of standing by to help. Even in the case of molluscs, when the cuttlefish is struck with the trident the male stands by to help the female; but when the male is struck the female runs away.

—Aristotle

ON THE PLACE OF DUPLICITY IN THE GREAT CHAIN OF BEING

Man is the only animal that can remain on friendly terms with the victims he intends to eat until he eats them. *—Samuel Butler*

A SMITHSONIAN INSTITUTE KIND OF THING?

Man seems to be a rickety sort of thing, any way you take him; a kind of British Museum of infirmities and interiorities. He is always undergoing repairs. A machine that was as unreliable as he is would have no market. *—Mark Twain*

WELL, THERE'S ALWAYS SANITARY ENGINEERING

Man, an ingenious assembly of portable plumbing.

—Christopher Morley

ON JUST HOW LONELY IT GETS UP THERE AT THE TOP

A man with a career can have no time to waste upon his wife and friends; he has to devote it wholly to his enemies.   *—John Oliver Hobbes*

BUT IT DOES HAVE ITS PERKS

Ever notice that the Jolly Green Giant stands around laughing his head off while the little people do all the work canning the vegetables?

—from The Best of Bridge

ON WHAT MIGHT PERHAPS BE
TOO OFTEN THE CASE

A husband should not insult his wife publicly, at parties. He should insult her in the privacy of the home.

—*James Thurber*

ON WHERE ALL THAT STUFF
ABOUT "MARGINAL MAN"
COMES FROM

Y'know the problem with men? After the birth, we're irrelevant.

—*Dustin Hoffman*

AND MAYBE THAT STUFF ABOUT
THE PRIMAL SCREAM

The majority of husbands remind me of an orangutan trying to play the violin.

—*Honoré de Balzac*

ON THE ROLE OF MARRIAGE
IN POLITICS

No man is regular in his attendance at the House of Commons until he is married.

—*Benjamin Disraeli*

ON WHAT TO LOOK FOR,
AESTHETICALLY SPEAKING

The beauty of stature is the only beauty of men.

—*Montaigne*

ON WHAT TO LOOK FOR, ON A
MORE PRAGMATIC LEVEL

A man should be taller, older, heavier, uglier, and hoarser than his wife.

—*Edgar Watson Howe*

ON JUST WHO THAT MIGHT
TURN OUT TO BE

I would like to be remembered—well, the Mexicans have an expression, *feo, fuerte y formal,* which means: He was ugly, was strong, and had dignity.

—John Wayne

ON THE DARK SECRET OF
HOLDING ONTO POWER

Men build bridges and throw railroads across deserts, and yet they contend successfully that the job of sewing on a button is beyond them. Accordingly, they don't have to sew buttons.

—Heywood Brown

ON PERFECTION BEING
WHERE YOU FIND IT

American women expect to find in their husbands a perfection that English women only hope to find in their butlers.

—W. Somerset Maugham

ON THE TRAGIC VISION

All women become like their mothers. That is their tragedy. No man does . . . that's his.

—Oscar Wilde

ON TRUTH—A ROUGH AND
TUMBLE APPROACH

Every man has a right to utter what he thinks is truth, and every other man has a right to knock him down for it. *—Samuel Johnson*

TRUTH RECONSIDERED IN
THE LIGHT OF DAY

A man has no more right to *say* an
uncivil thing than to *act* one; no
more right to say a rude thing to
another than to knock him down.

—*Samuel Johnson*

ON THE TRUTH THAT FOLLOWS
CONSEQUENCE

If men could get pregnant, abortion
would be sacrament.

—*Laura Sabia, National Action
Committee on the Status of Women*

OH COME ON NOW, IS IT
REALLY THAT BAD?

He who hates vice hates men.

—*John Morley*

ON THE SALUBRIOUS EFFECTS OF THE IMPULSE TO WAR

Men love war because it allows them to look serious; because it is the only thing that stops women laughing at them.

—John Fowles

AN OLD, SAD STORY

Once there were two brothers. One ran away to sea, the other was elected Vice-President and nothing was heard of either of them.

—Thomas R. Marshall

ON QUITTING WHILE STILL AHEAD

If a man understands one woman he should let it go at that.

—Calgary Bob Edwards, 1912

FOR EVERY
SILVER LINING

People are always ready to admit a
man's ability after he gets there.

—Calgary Bob Edwards

THERE'S ALWAYS THE
CLOUDY PART

A man is very apt to complain of the
ingratitude of those who have risen
above him.

—Samuel Johnson

SEEK AND YE SHALL
PROBABLY FIND

A good man who goes wrong is just
a bad man who has been found out.

—Calgary Bob Edwards

ON MALE SUFFERAGE AND
THE DOMINO EFFECT

Another trouble is that if men start to vote, they will vote too much. Politics unsettles men, and unsettled men mean unsettled bills—broken furniture, broken vows, and divorce . . .

—*Nellie McClung, 1914*

AMONG OTHER QUESTIONS
RESERVED FOR THE ALMIGHTY

Why is the careless, easy-going, irresponsible way of the young girl so attractive to men? It does not make for domestic happiness; and why, oh why, do some of our best men marry such odd little sticks of pinhead women, with a brain similar in calibre to a second-rate butterfly, while the most intelligent, unselfish, and womanly women are left un-mated? I am going to ask about this the first morning I am in heaven.

—*Nellie McClung*

ON CARRYING PUBLISHING INITIATIVES INTO PUBLIC LIFE

Formerly we used to canonize our heroes. The modern method is to vulgarize them. Cheap editions of great books may be delightful, but cheap editions of great men are absolutely detestable.

—*Oscar Wilde, The Critic as Artist*

UNSAVOURY ASPECTS OF THE LITERARY LIFE

Ruined by a book! Such was my awful fate. Henry Miller had no effect on me; D.H. Lawrence left me cold; I yawned my way through Frank Harris' memoirs. But then I came across a copy of Eaton's catalogue: and, leafing idly through it, discovered photographs of men wearing full-length winter undergarments.

—*Richard J. Needham, 1960*

OR IS THAT ALL TOO OFTEN THE PROBLEM?

Divide your attention equally between men and books.

—*Sir William Osler, 1905*

ON TAKING THE SENSIBLE APPROACH

There are no perfect men of course, but some are more perfect than

others, and we can use all of those
we can get.

—Merle Shain, 1973

ON A FATHER'S DREAM
FOR HIS NEW-BORN SON

I want him to be a man's man.
—Prince Philip

ON RONALD REAGAN'S WORST
DREAM ABOUT
HIS GROWN-UP SON

He's all man—we made sure of that.
—Ronald Reagan

ON THE SIDE EFFECTS OF
LIVING IN INSTITUTIONS
ALL ONE'S LIFE

Why do you think I'm getting married? I'll tell you it's because I've

never really had a home. From the time I was eight I've always been away at school or in the navy.

—*Prince Philip*

ON THE ROLE OF IMAGINATION IN A GENDER-SPECIFIC WORLD

Women have more imagination than men. They need it to tell us how wonderful we are.

—*Arnold H. Glasgow*

ON WHAT IS ALL TOO OFTEN THE CASE

He is every other inch a gentleman.

—*Rebecca West*

ON THE OLD BINARY EXCLUSION PRINCIPLE

I go for two kinds of men. The kind

with muscles and the kind without.
—*Mae West*

ON THE OTHER SIDE
OF THE COIN

It is hard to be a man in a field dominated by women. Like the token woman, I am under great pressure to be above average.
—*Ralph A. Dowling, secretary*

HISTORICAL DETERMINISM
PROVES IRRESISTIBLE

The first thing to recognize is that despite all the talk about equality men are different from women. The most important difference (after the anatomical and obvious) is that men can't do anything alone. This is basic. It's been like that since they went off together in packs to hunt, while women stayed alone and swept the cave. It's been reinforced by the Industrial Age. One man turns the bolt while the other man holds the nut. It's in the union contract .

—*Barbara Holland*

ON SOMETHING OF SOCIAL VALUE AND NOT SEX OBJECTS

We don't pose men as sex objects. We think of it more as something of social value.

—*Toni Holt, Playgirl magazine*

ON THE SIDE EFFECTS OF THE NEGLECT OF DOMESTIC DUTIES

The home seems to me to be the proper sphere for the man. And certainly once a man begins to neglect his domestic duties, he becomes painfully effeminate, does he not? And I don't like that. It makes men so very attractive.

—*Oscar Wilde*

ON WHAT DOESN'T FIT, WHATEVER THAT MEANS

But a truly feminine man, like a truly masculine woman, will never do. It doesn't fit and it's self-destructing.

—*Cecil Beaton*

ON WHAT ENGLAND NEEDS

Boy George is all England needs—another queen who can't dress.

—*Joan Rivers*

JUST ONE OF A THOUSAND
DIFFERENT WAYS

Males have made asses of themselves writing about the female sexual experience.

—William H. Masters

AND STILL MAYBE NOT
ALL THERE IS TO IT

To tell about a drunken muzhik's beating his wife is incomparably harder than to compose a whole tract about the "woman question."

—Turgenev

ON WHAT TO REMEMBER WHEN
ALL ELSE FAILS

Watch out for men who have mothers.

—Laura Shapiro

ON WHAT TO REMEMBER
BEFORE ALL ELSE FAILS

Don't accept rides from strange men, and remember that all men are as strange as hell.

—Robin Morgan

ON THE THING THAT
NOT EVEN PRACTICE
MAKES PERFECT

Having practiced for hours in front of the mirror, I can work up a fairly ferocious expression, but I have not got, and never will have, a natural-born fighting face.

—Lt.-Gen. George S. Patton

ON WHAT
PRACTICE MAKES
NEARLY PERFECT

Tell him you love his body. If you choke on that phrase, practice until it comes out naturally. If you haven't admired him lately, he's probably starving emotionally. He can't take too much at once, so start slowly. Give him one good compliment a day and watch him blossom right before your eyes.

—*Marabel Morgan,*
The Total Woman, 1973

ON THE VIRTUE OF HAVING A
SECOND CHANCE

First time you buy a house you see how pretty the paint is and buy it. The second time you look to see if the basement has termites. It's the same with men.

—*Lupe Velez, 1977*

LITTLE-KNOWN FACT
OF INTEREST

Some of them are really manly and you'll never dream they were queer. Not from the look of them. But I can always tell 'cos they've all got LPs of Judy Garland.

—*Joe Orton*

ARGUMENT FOR IMPROVED
FUNDING OF PUBLIC LIBRARIES

The writing on men's room walls is among the finest this country has produced.

—*Boyd McDonald*

ON THE ROLE OF SEXUAL PREFERENCE IN THE HISTORY OF ART AND RELIGION

If Michelangelo were a heterosexual, the Sistine Chapel would have been painted basic white and with a roller.

—*Rita Mae Brown*

HARD FACTS ABOUT SOFT GUYS

Indulgent male inverts like pleasant, artistic things, and nearly all of them are fond of music. They also like praise and admiration. They are poor whistlers. Their favourite colour is green.

—*John F.W. Meagher, psychiatrist, 1929*

NIETSCHE'S WORST NIGHTMARE

Look, I'm Superman!

—Pierre Trudeau

MAYBE GOOD FOR THOSE OTHER GUYS, TOO

It is a good thing for the uneducated man to read books of quotations.

—Winston Churchill

JUST HOW MANY SHIRTS HAVE YOU GOT?

I wish I could change my sex as I change my shirt.

—André Breton

NEVER BE AFRAID TO STRETCH YOUR METAPHORS

Boys marry because of a chronic ir-ritation that causes them to gravitate

in the direction of objects with certain curvilinear properties.
—*Ashley Montague*

WHEN ALL ELSE FAILS, TRY A NON-SEQUITER

Man is about to become a woman.
—*Marshall McLuhan*

ON GETTING THROUGH THOSE LONG WINTERS WHILE AVOIDING REVULSION

If a guy wants to wear his hair down to his ass, I'm not revolted by it. But I don't look at him and say, 'Now there's a fella I'd like to spend next winter with.'
—*John Wayne*

ON THE ROAD SO SADLY NOT TO HAVE BEEN TRAVELLED BY

Imagine me going around with a pot belly. It would mean political ruin.

—*Adolf Hitler*

EARLY VENTURE INTO GAMING THEORY

Man is a gaming animal, he must always be trying to get the better in something or other.

—*Charles Lamb*

STILL HOLDING 150 YEARS LATER

It is necessary for me to establish a winner image. Therefore, I have to beat somebody.

—*Richard Nixon, 1968*

YEAH, BUT HE'S PROBABLY DRUNK

Any man who hates small dogs and children can't be all bad.

—W. C. Fields

NOT TO MENTION SOME KIND OF CONTROL-FREAK

Marriage is a two-way proposition, but never let the woman know she is one of the two ways.

—W. C. Fields

ON THE POWER OF IMAGES

Every man I've known has fallen in love with Gilda and wakened with me.

—Rita Hayworth, after starring in Gilda

GREY FLANNEL NEED NOT APPLY

I don't want my editors marrying

anyone and getting a lot of foolish notions in their heads about 'togetherness,' home, family and all that jazz.

—*Hugh Hefner*

ON RISKING WIMPINESS: THE ARGUMENT FOR ART

If it is fun to daub paint on a canvas, go ahead and do it and let the other guys sneer!

—*Today's Health,1957*

DISCOURSE ON THE BIOLOGICAL SPRINGS OF NON-WIMPINESS

—Men, what is the spirit of the bayonet?

—To kill, drill sergeant.

—Men, will you kill?

—Yes, drill sergeant.

—Men, why will you kill?
—Because we have balls, drill sergeant.

—*US Marine chant*

WHAT'S THE USE OF
CORRECT THINKING?

I've been married to a Fascist and
married to a Marxist and neither one
of them took out the garbage.

—*anonymous celebrity*

ON THE SADLY OBVIOUS

A masculine movement without
qualification must be claimed by
men.

—*Joseph Goebbels*

ON FORTITUDE IN HIGH OFFICE

My arm is like granite—rigid and

unbending. But Goring can't stand it. He has to drop his arm after half an hour of this salute. He's flabby, but I am hard.

—*Adolf Hitler*

ON VIRTUE IN
HIGH OFFICE

I was tougher than you were in World War II and I'm tougher than you are now!

—*Robert McNamara*

ON THE ROLE OF BASEBALL
IN THE LIFE OF REAL BOYS

All boys love baseball. If they don't, they're not real boys.

—*Zane Grey*

ON THE ROLE OF BASEBALL
IN THE LIVES OF REAL PEOPLE

Baseball is very big with my people. It figures. It's the only time we can get to shake a bat at a white man without starting a riot.

—*Dick Gregory*

ON BASEBALL AND WHAT IT'S
COME TO WITH THOSE PLASTIC
BLOW-UP DOLLS

You come here to watch the game. You don't really need to see men sucking on women's parts, even if they're plastic.

—*Jeannine Robbins,*
baseball spectator, 1991

ON TRAINING BOYS FOR
LIFE—PREFERRED TECHNIQUES

Except for war, there is nothing in the American life, nothing, which trains a boy better for life than football.

—Robert Kennedy

SECOND THOUGHTS ON
THE SPORTING LIFE

Is it normal to wake up in the morning in a sweat because you can't wait to beat another human's guts out?

—Joe Kapp, former quarterback

ON THE QUALIFICATIONS OF
THE SUPREME BEING

The Yale President must be a Yale man. Not too far to the right, too far to the left or a middle-of-the-roader.

You may have guessed who the leading candidate is but there is a question about him: Is God a Yale man?

—*Wilmorth S. Lewis*

ON WHO WEARS THE PANTS, AND
THE CONSEQUENCES THEREOF

I do, and I also wash and iron them.

—*Denis Thatcher*

AND DON'T FORGET
THE TOWELS, THE UNDERWEAR
—AND THE SOCKS!

Yes, if ironed sheets mean so much to your husband, it's worth 30 minutes a week to make him happy.

—*Ann Landers*

LAST WORD ON IRONING

O men, with sisters dear!
O men, with mothers and wives!
It is not linen you're wearing out,
but human creatures' lives!
　　—*Thomas Hood, 'The Song of the Shirt'*

OF MEN AND MICE

Women do not like timid men. Cats
do not like prudent mice.
　　　　　　　　—*H. L. Mencken*

OF YIN AND YANG

There aren't any hard women, only
soft men.
　　　　　　　　—*Raquel Welch*

LAST WORD ON PENIS ENVY

When I was in the ballet world I
went through another period where

I wished I was a boy because I wanted somebody to ask me out on a date.

—*Madonna*

THE QUESTION NO ONE
SHOULD HAVE TO ASK

To whom do I appeal when the executioner is my judge?

—*Middle Eastern women's proverb*

ASPECTS OF
A MAN'S LIFE

Myself, my brother, my father, and my cousin against the world. Myself, my brother, and my father against my cousin. Myself and my brother against my father. Myself against my brother.

—*Palestinian men's proverb*

SOUNDS LIKE A
PRETTY BORING PLACE,
WHEN YOU STOP TO THINK

I myself shall lead her, in order to make her male, so that she too may become a living spirit resembling you males. For every woman who will make herself male will enter the Kingdom of Heaven.

—*Jesus, The Gospel of Thomas (c. 140 CE)*

TRY NOT TO GET TOO TEDIOUS
ON THIS ONE, EH?

Man eternally creates woman. Man is eternally born out of his own creation.

—*Mel Lyman*

IN FACT, NOW THAT YOU MENTION IT

I wish Adam had died with all his ribs in his body.

—Dion Boucicault

ON THE TOTAL MAN —A REALITY CHECK

I'm totally a man. And when I go into the bathroom in the morning, I'm quite aware of what I am.

—Boy George

AFTER A HARD DAY IN HIGH OFFICE —ANOTHER REALITY CHECK

Well, I've gotta take ol' Jumbo here and give him some exercise. I wonder who I'll fuck tonight.

—Lyndon B. Johnson

ON WHAT ISN'T EASY
FOR MERE MAN

Well, it's hard for a mere man to believe that woman doesn't have equal rights.

—Dwight Eisenhower

LAST WORD ON THE SEARCH
FOR MISTER RIGHT

An archeologist is the best husband any woman can have: the older she gets, the more interested he is in her.

—Agatha Christie

ON HAVING HOME A MAN
THE FAMILY IN

My wife and I are just exactly like many thousands of other families in America today. We have home our son, and what is far more important

... our grandchildren have home
their daddy.
—*Dwight D. Eisenhower, U.S. President*

ON THE BINARY OPPOSITION AT
THE HEART OF THINGS

The father is always a Republican
toward his son, and his mother's
always a democrat.   —*Robert Frost*

PRAYER FOR THE CONSTRUCTION
OF YET ANOTHER TIN GOD

Build me a son, O Lord, who will be
strong enough to know when he is
weak, and brave enough to face
himself when he is afraid, one who
will be proud and unbending in
honest defeat, and humble and gen-
tle in victory.

—*Gen. Douglas MacArthur*

ON THE DEBIT SIDE
OF CREDIT

The fundamental defect of fathers is
that they want their children to be a
credit to them.

—*Bertrand Russell*

CAREFUL TO STOP JUST
THIS SIDE OF QUICHE

My father was determined to turn
my brother into some sort of his idea
of a man, and that included a man
who eats chicken.

—*Roseanne Barr*

MEANWHILE, ON THE BLEAKER
EXISTENTIAL SIDE

A man in love is incomplete until he
is married. Then he is finished.

—*Zsa Zsa Gabor*

ON THE STRANGELY CONVINCING
POWER OF NONSENSE

I believe that the husband should be the head of the household, that he should be the boss . . . I know it's nonsense to believe that a woman doesn't have the same natural instincts and shouldn't have the same rights as a man, but that's the way I was brought up . . .

—*James Caan*

YOU PROBABLY HAVE
TO BE THERE

I love it when men say 'fock' in New York, and I love it when they say it to me in New York.

—*Roseanne Barr*

ON THE ILLUSORY NATURE OF
THE NEW AND IMPROVED DUDE

You're fooling yourself if you think you've got new and improved males because you see three or four dudes out there doing diapers and dishes.

—Bill Cosby

ON SEEING WHAT YOU WANT TO
SEE, EVEN WHEN THEY ARE
JUST-RELEASED PRISONERS OF WAR

It was a very moving experience to see their wives and the two of them—gaunt, lean, quiet, confident, with enormous faith in the country, in God, and in themselves.

—Richard Nixon

ON MAINTAINING A GOOD
COLLAR-AND-LEASH
RELATIONSHIP

Generally speaking, a man who has a satisfactory physical relationship with his wife will not slip his collar and seek extra-marital affairs.

—Ann Landers

ON WHY UTOPIA CONTINUES TO
ELUDE THE SPECIES

Man should be trained for war and woman for the recreation of the warrior.

—Nietzsche

ON THE RIGOURS OF BEING A MAN

When a stupid man is doing something he is ashamed of, he always declares that it is his duty.

—George Bernard Shaw, 1898

ON MAINTAINING AN OPTIMISTIC POSITION

I refuse to consign the whole male sex to the nursery. I insist on believing that some men are my equals.

—*Brigid Brophy*

POSSIBLY NOT THAT HARD TO FIND

I require only three things of a man. He must be handsome, ruthless, and stupid.

—*Dorothy Parker*

MORE ON THE BINARY EXCLUSION THING

I like two kinds of men: domestic and foreign.

—*Mae West*

THOUGHTS ON THE KEY TO THE GREAT CODE OF LIFE

Men are like ciphers ... they acquire their value merely from their position.

—*Napoleon Bonaparte*

YOU CAN TAKE THE GENERAL OUT OF THE COUNTRY, BUT YOU CAN'T TAKE THE GENERAL OUT OF THE GENERAL

All Norm ever wanted was to be a good soldier. He's very patriotic. He loves parades and rituals of all kinds. Take Christmas. When he sent gifts home last Christmas from Riyadh they were in color-coded wrapping and came with a list of how to give them out.

—*Brenda Schwartzkopf, 1991*

ON WHAT HAPPENS
TO FORTITUDE

Back where I come from, we have men we call heroes. Once a year they take their fortitude out of mothballs to parade it down the main street.

—*The Wizard of Oz*

ON WHAT IT'S LIKE TO HAVE A
REAL MAN AROUND THE HOUSE

When Norm sets his mind to do something, he always does it well. He's a terrific magician. One of his favourites—I hate this one—it's an arm cutter that's like a guillotine thing that you stick your hand in.

—*Brenda Schwartzkopf, 1991*

ON HEROES AND FRIENDS

Of course, he is my hero. He is a

tower of strength for me. He is my best friend.
—*Brenda Schwartzkopf, People, 1991*

ON WHAT, WHEN YOU REALLY THINK ABOUT IT, WE NEED THE LEAST OF

We don't need another hero.
—*Tina Turner*

SPEAK FOR YOURSELF, ERNIE

The better you treat a man and the more you show him you love him, the quicker he gets tired of you.
—*Ernest Hemingway, To Have and Have Not*

SAME GOES FOR YOU, OSCAR

There's nothing in the world like the devotion of a married woman. It's a

thing no married man knows anything about.

—*Oscar Wilde*

ON THE ADVANTAGES OF BOYS
NEVER CEASING TO BE BOYS

It's a real advantage having a bully
[Harvie Andre] trying to run the
House [of Commons]. His temper
tantrums give my guys a shot of
adrenalin.

—*Jean-Robert Gauthier,*
Liberal House Leader, 1990

ON THE SALUBRIOUS EFFECTS OF
EXPECTING WAR

My staff and I had a war cabinet
meeting twice a week: that was
good fun.

—*Harvie Andre, 1990*

ON FATUOUSNESS KNOWING NO LIMITS IN POLITICS OR WAR

Fight on my men, I am hurt but I am not slain; I'll lay me down and bleed a while, and then I'll rise and fight again.

—*Jean Chretien, Liberal Party leader*

LITTLE-KNOWN SECRET TO TRAVELLING IN CHINA

In the countryside, ask questions about directions etc. of men. Women probably won't know the answers.

—*Elizabeth Devine, travel writer*

SURE, ERROL, BUT THEN WHO DOESN'T?

I love a man who can best me.

—*Errol Flynn*

ON SECOND THOUGHT, THOUGH

There is no glory in outstripping donkeys.

—Martial, AD 70

DOES HE SAY "AW SHUCKS" ALL THE TIME?

People are tired of getting screwed by everything and everybody, and in my pictures, I like to play this character who's not quite all there, who steps down from his truck and scrapes the manure off his boots and who's always fighting for his dignity. He's anti-establishment, he's funny and he's somebody to cheer for—a hero.

—Burt Reynolds

ON STRAIGHTENING OUT THE STRAIGHTS: THE AFFIRMATIVE ACTION APPROACH

Well, straight men need to be emasculated. They all need to be slapped around. Every straight guy should have a man's tongue in his mouth at least once. —*Madonna*

ON DEMOCRACY AND THE GREAT MAN IN HISTORY

One man with courage makes a majority. —*Andrew Jackson, 1832*

WELL, YOU MIGHT HAVE STARTED WITH UNIVERSAL SUFFRAGE THEN, EH?

We might as well require a man to wear still the coat which titled him as a boy, as civilized society to remain

ever under the regimen of their bar-
barous ancestors.

—Thomas Jefferson

MEDITATION ON WHAT
ALL MEN ARE EQUAL BEFORE

Fishing is the chance to wash one's
soul with pure air. It brings meek-
ness and inspiration, reduces our
egotism, soothes our troubles and
shames our wickedness. It is discip-
line in the equality of men—for all
men are equal before the fish.

—Herbert Hoover

ON WHY FISHING APPEALS TO THE
MAN IN HIGH OFFICE

There is a pleasure and, above all, a
peace to be enjoyed in fishing far
beyond anything else I know; it is as

if the outside world were forbidden to intrude upon a fisherman's thoughts.

—*John Diefenbaker*

YEAH, BUT WHO TELLS THE LIES?

History makes the man more than the man makes history.

—*Richard Nixon*

A PROBLEM OF BULK

The bulk of mankind are schoolboys through life.

—*Thomas Jefferson*

ON TAKING FALSE ANALOGIES JUST ABOUT AS FAR AS YOU CAN

The man who loves other countries as much as his own stands on a level with the man who loves other

women as much as he loves his own
wife.   —*Theodore Roosevelt*

WHILE FORGETTING THE
OLD CURMUDGEON

Patriotism is the last refuge of a
scoundrel.   —*Samuel Johnson*

ON THE CONTINUED PERSISTENCE
OF THE WYATT EARP SYNDROME

Arms alone are not enough to keep
the peace. It must be kept by men.
            —*John F. Kennedy*

ON THE SALUBRIETY OF
THE ONLY KIND OF WAR

A just war is in the long run far
better for a man's soul than the most
prosperous peace.

            —*Theodore Roosevelt*

DON'T GO SOFT ON US NOW, TEDDY

We do not admire the men of timid peace.

—Theodore Roosevelt

ON HAVING A POWERFUL POLITICIAN FOR A FATHER

He seemed to me a very powerful man. He could order the fathers of other boys into battle and could produce jam.

—Randolph S. Churchill

SOME SAY IT WAS REALLY THE JAM

My most brilliant achievement was my ability to be able to persuade my wife to marry me.

—Winston Churchill

ON THE RUB THAT LIES AT
THE BOTTOM OF IT ALL

There is no good father, that's the rule. Don't lay the blame on men but on the bond of paternity, which is rotten.

—*Jean-Paul Sartre*

ON THE INEFFABLE BONDS
OF PATERNITY

My father was frightened of his father, I was frightened of my father, and I am damned well going to see to it that my children are frightened of me.

—*King George V*

ON WHAT NOT TO SAY AT THE CORNER TAVERN, MINUTES BEFORE CLOSING TIME

The American is hysterical about his manhood.

—*Gore Vidal*

OH, FOR THEM GOOD OLD DAYS

Real men are a dying breed in this country. There aren't any John Waynes any more—in show business or on the outside; it's all over; all you've got now walking around is a bunch of sissies.

—*Mike Connors*

ON WHAT IT MUST BE THAT SLIGHTLY MAIMS A MAN

A man who is not interested in

women is in some ways a little
maimed.   —*Edith Cresson,*
                    Prime Minister of France, 1991

MORE ON THE GREAT
MAN SYNDROME

Behind every great man stands an
amazed mother-in-law.
                    —*from The Best of Bridge*

ON THE INEVITABLE
PROCESSES OF EVOLUTION

The penis is obviously going the
way of the vermiform appendix.
                    —*Jill Johnston, American feminist*

ON THE PROTECTIONIST SYNDROME

Every man I meet wants to protect
me. Can't figure out from whom.
                    —*Mae West*

WELL, YOU MIGHT LOOK AT IT THIS WAY

Give a man a free hand and he'll run it all over you.

—*Mae West*

A FAMILIAR SCENARIO

Basically my wife was immature. I'd be at home in the bath and she'd come in and sink my boats.

—*Woody Allen*

STILL SOME HOPE THEN? ON THE REHABILITATION OF JOHN HINCKLEY, WOULD-BE ASSASSIN OF RONALD REAGAN

He's come to realize this was an inappropriate way to impress a girl.

—*Frederick Schwartz, attorney*

WHAT WAS IT THAT CALLED THE
KETTLE SOMETHING SIMILAR?

No man is such a liar as the indignant man.

—*Nietzsche*

ON THE CASE FOR
GENETIC ENGINEERING

Men are generally more careful of the breed of their horses and dogs than of their children

—*William Penn, founder of Pennsylvania*

ETERNAL IMPEDIMENTS TO
A MAN'S CAREER

Music and women I cannot but give way to, whatever my business is.

—*Samuel Pepys, 1666*

ON DRINKING ONESELF
TOWARD HEROISM

Claret is the liquor for boys, port for men; but he who aspires to be a hero must drink brandy.

—*Samuel Johnson*

WORDS UTTERED ONLY
TO BE EATEN

I am very fond of the company of ladies. I like their beauty, I like their delicacy, I like their vivacity, and I like their silence.   —*Samuel Johnson*

ON VOLITIONALITY
AND GREATNESS

A man of genius makes no mistakes. His errors are volitional and are the portals of discovery.

—*James Joyce, Ulysses*

CAN WE TRY THAT AGAIN WITHOUT THE BIG WORDS?

The greatest men are always linked to their age by some weakness or other.   —*Johann Wolfgang von Goethe*

ACHILLES HEEL TRANSMUTED

A man's an awful coward when his pants begin to go.   —*Henry Lawson*

ON ATTAINING RESPECTABILITY

The more things a man is ashamed of, the more respectable he is.
—*George Bernard Shaw*

ON MADNESS, HUMILITY AND FOLLY

Provided a man is not mad, he can be cured of every folly but vanity.
—*Jean Jacques Rousseau*

FINALLY, A SOLID
PIECE OF ADVICE

When I leave home to walk to school
Dad always says to me,
'Marco keep your eyelids up
and see what you can see.'

—Dr. Seuss

IMAGINE IT *NOW*, WITH
EXTENDED-PLAY CDS

A man is like a phonograph with
half-a-dozen records. You soon get
tired of them all; and yet you have to
sit at table while he reels them off to
every new visitor.

—George Bernard Shaw

ON THERE BEING SOME SMALL HOPE (IF YOU'VE GOT THE TECHNOLOGY)

No man is totally depraved who can spend half an hour by himself playing with his little boy's electric train.
—*Simeon Strunsky*

ON NOT REALLY NEEDING TO HAVE THE LAST WORD

Why are women so much more interesting to men than men are to women?

—*Virginia Woolf*

AND NOW THE LONG DARK NIGHT OF THE SOUL

Decent clothes . . . a car, but what's it all about?

—*Michael Caine, in Alfie*

Index

OLINE LUINENBURG is an editor and a graduate student in Communications at Simon Fraser University, Vancouver.

STEPHEN OSBORNE is co-editor of *Quotations from Chairman Zalm* and publisher of Geist magazine.

LITTLE RED BOOKS

It is the purpose of Little Red Books to gather the essential wisdom of great men and women into single volumes so that students of the Great might judge them in light of their own words, and find where they will the spiritual models so earnestly sought after by the young, so often forgotten by the old.